A Notary's

The Ones I Did Not

&

Will Not

NOTARY

Jeannie Eunice Franks Belgrave

First Printing: 2018

ISBN 978-0-359-07549-2

Self Published. Year of our Lord 2018

PO Box 7170
Hampton, Virginia 23666
https://www.virginianotary.club

Ordering Information:

Special discounts are available on quantity purchases by corporations, associations, educators, and others. For details, contact the publisher at the above listed address or e-mail the publisher at myvirginianotary@gmail.com

U.S trade bookstores and wholesalers: please contact Jeannie Eunice Franks at myvirginianotary@gmail.com

Content written in this journal after it is bought or obtained by third parties or vendors belongs to the writer of that content.

A Notary's Journal

Dear Notary,

as you are aware of, the notarial acts recorded
are those notaries said "yes" to.

This journal gives you the opportunity to
express observations, feelings, and growth in
your notarial skills when you experienced
notarial moments where you had to say
"no" to the notarial act.

A notary public is also a human being
in continued growth. Each notarial act will
bring a unique expeirnce. This journal gives
you the oopportunity to record what the
Notary's LogBook or Book of Official Records
did not let you record such as
The Ones You Said Not To. Yours,

Jeannie Eunice Franks

A Notary's Journal

Date:

Place:

The One I said No To:

A Notary's Journal

A Notary's Journal

Date:

Place:

The One I said No To:

Date:

Place:

The One I said No To:

Date:

Place:

The One I said No To:

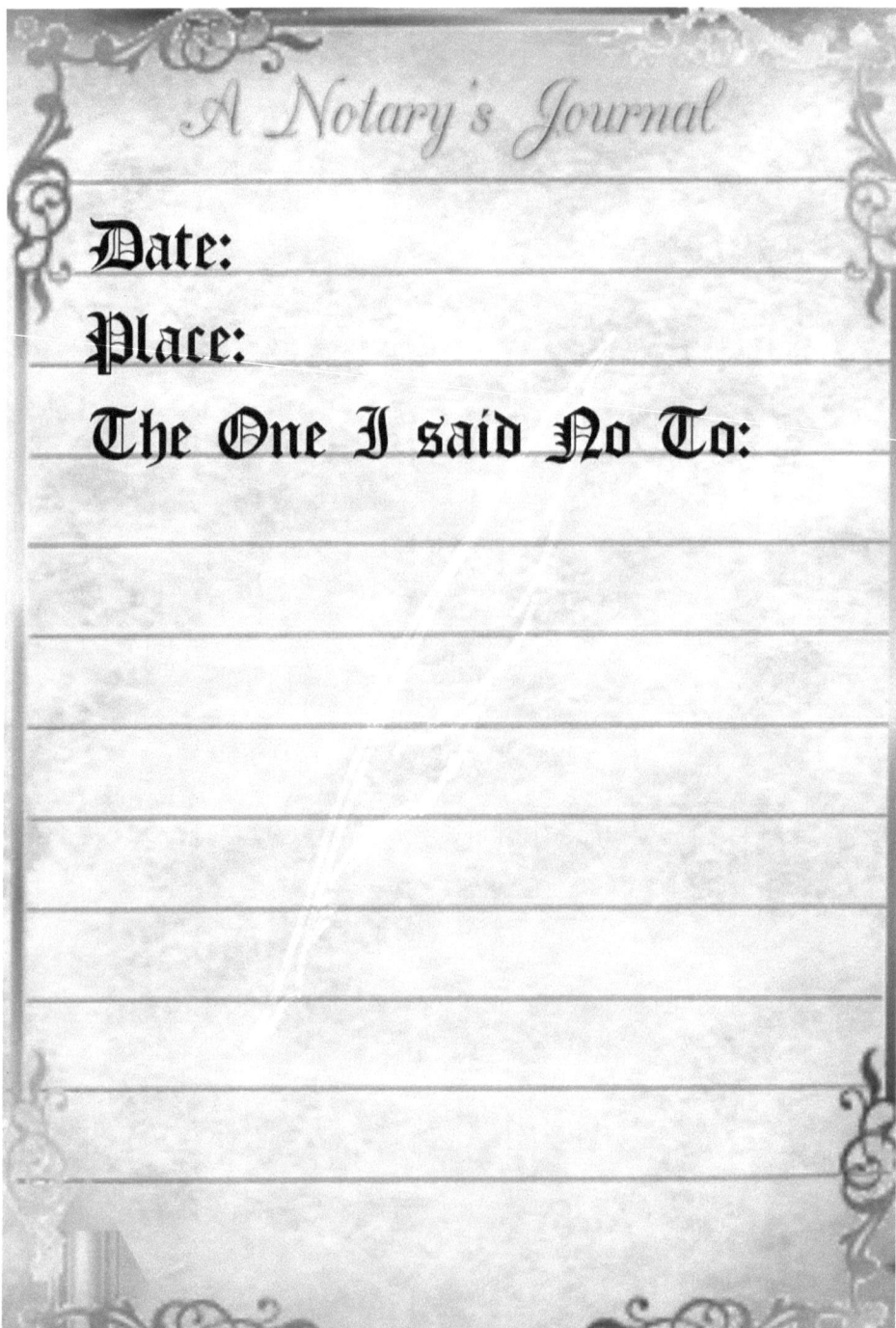

A Notary's Journal

Date:

Place:

The One I said No To:

Date:

Place:

The One I said No To:

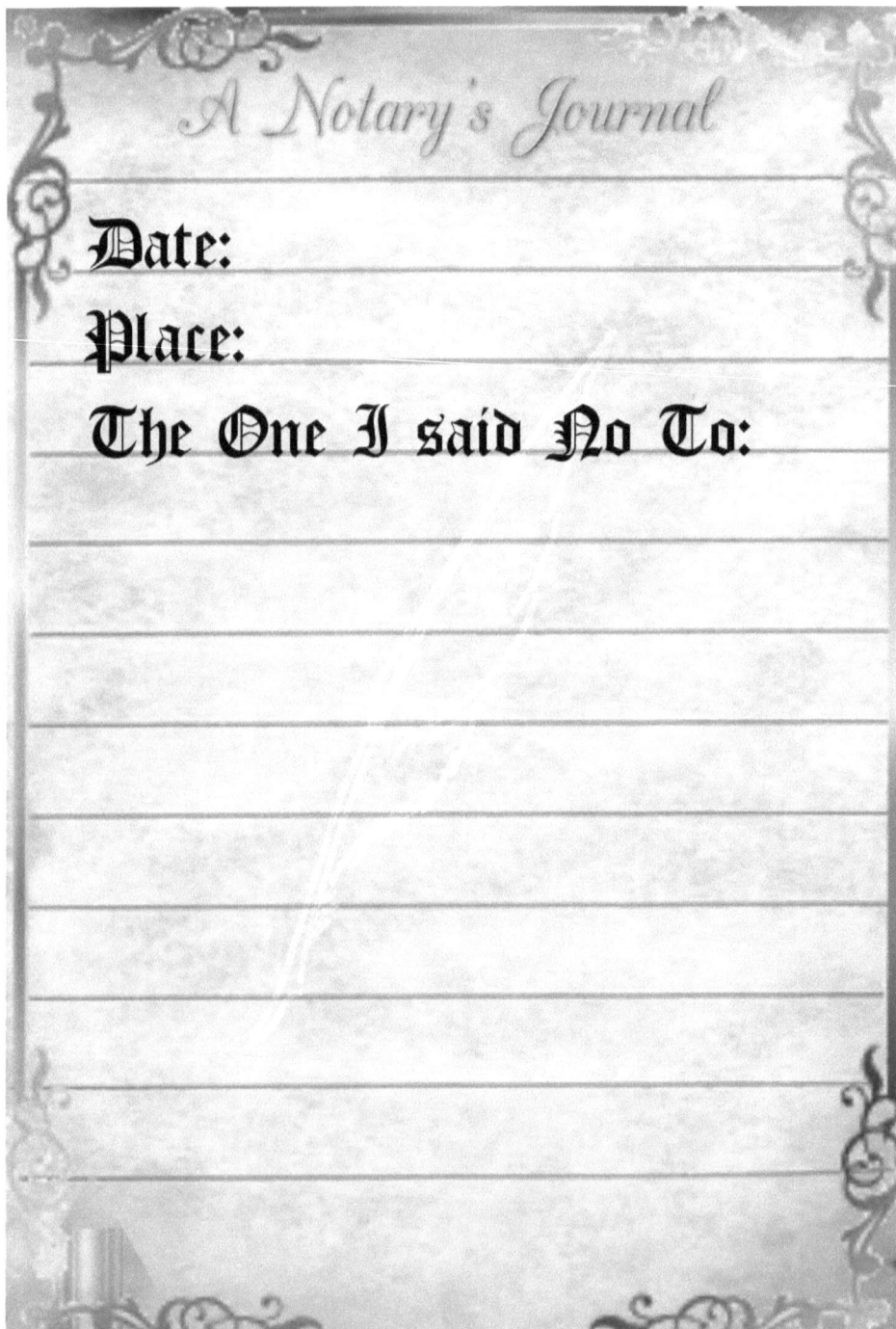

A Notary's Journal

Date:

Place:

The One I said No To:

Date:

Place:

The One I said No To:

A Notary's Journal

Date:

Place:

The One I said No To:

A Notary's Journal

Date:

Place:

The One I said No To:

A Notary's Journal

Date:

Place:

The One I said No To:

Date:

Place:

The One I said No To:

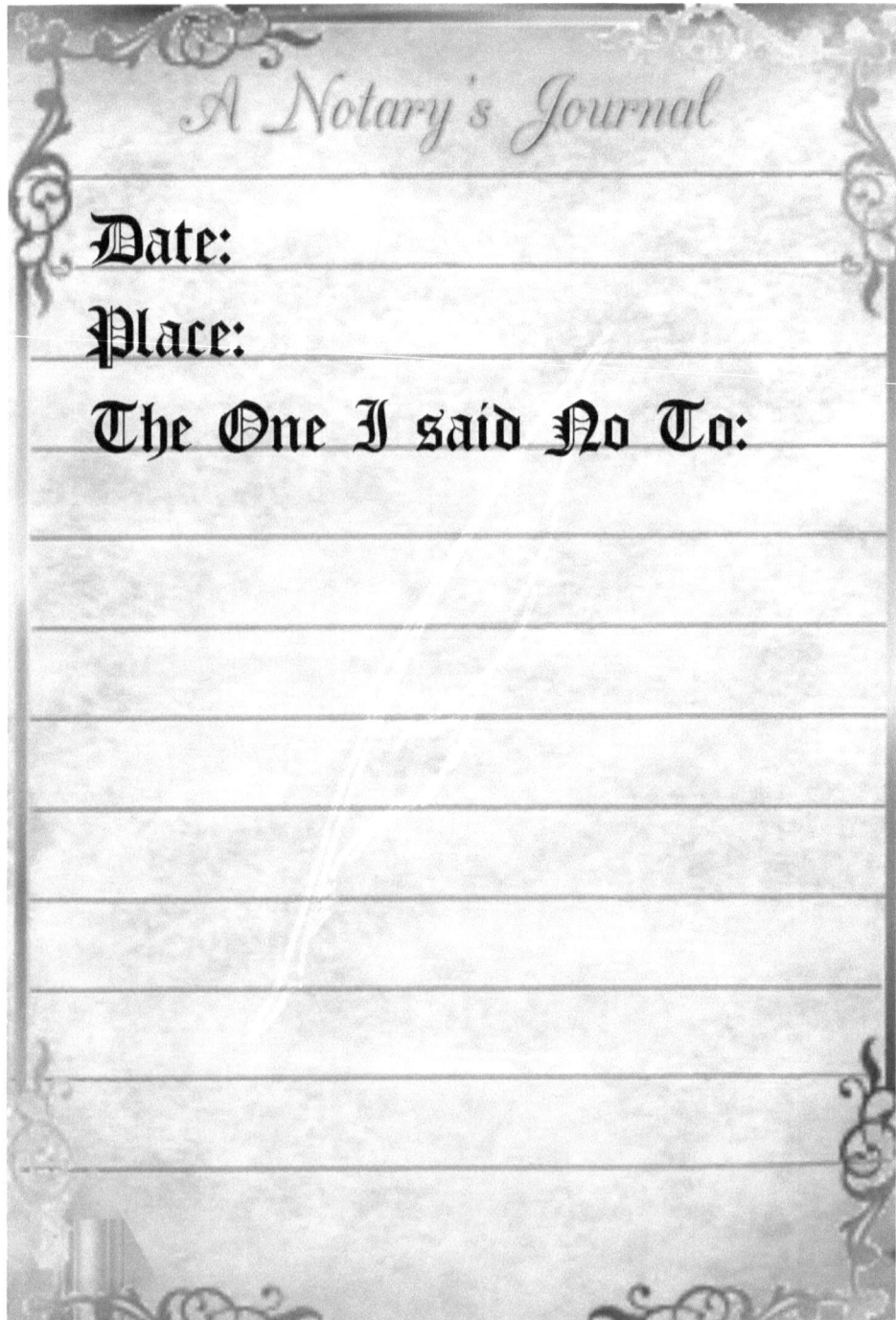

A Notary's Journal

Date:

Place:

The One I said No To:

Date:

Place:

The One I said No To:

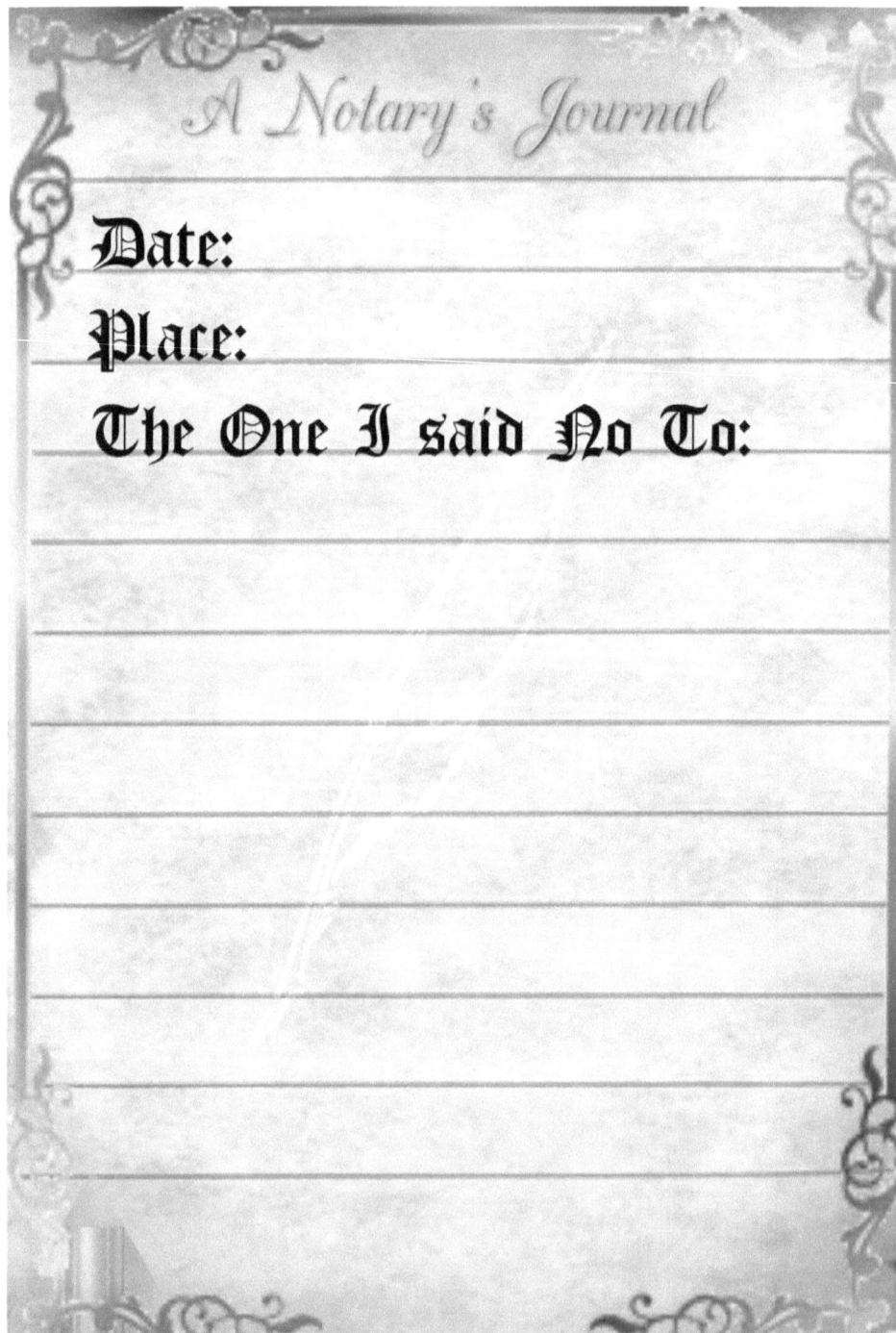

A Notary's Journal

Date:

Place:

The One I said No To:

Date:

Place:

The One I said No To:

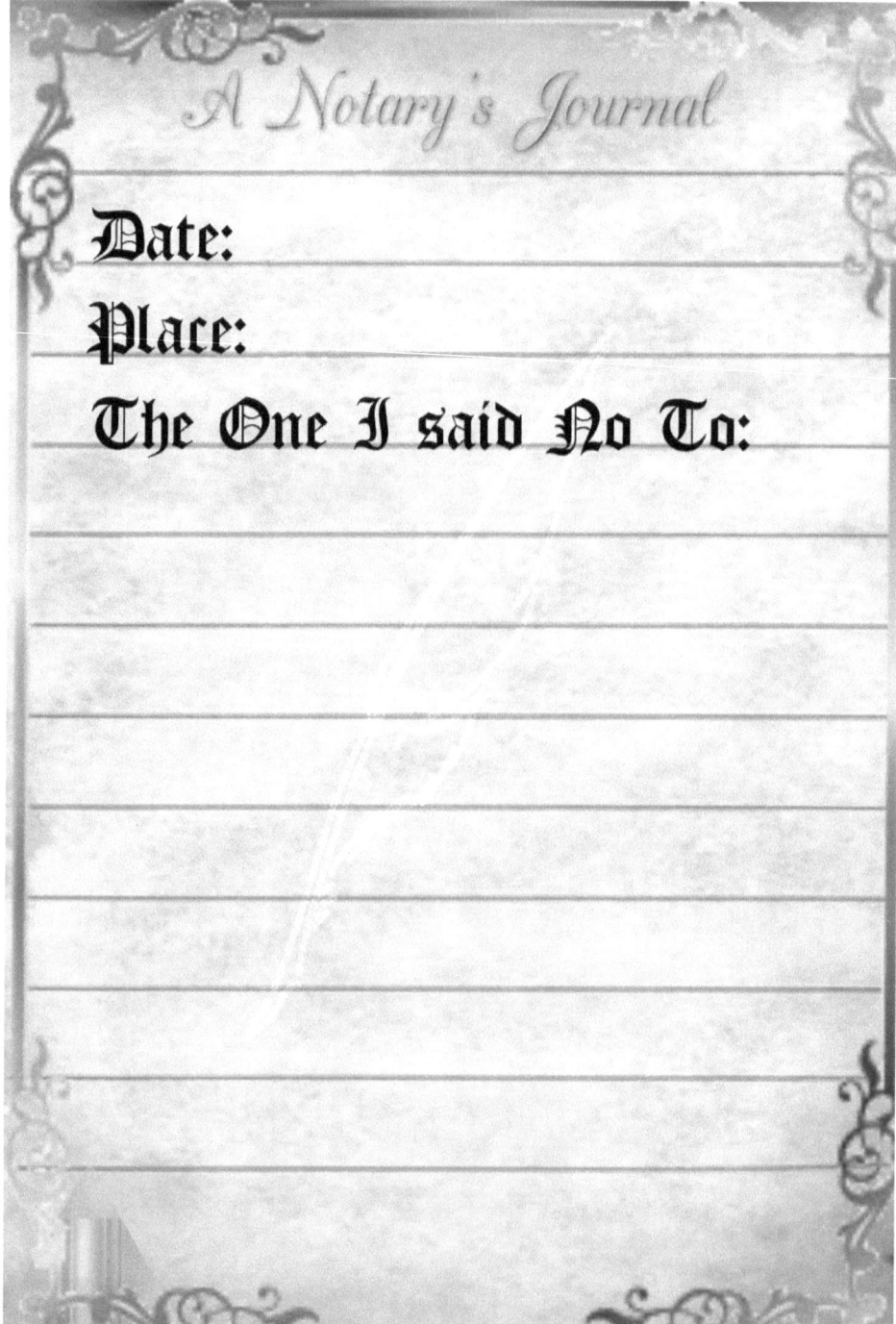

A Notary's Journal

Date:

Place:

The One I said No To:

Date:

Place:

The One I said No To:

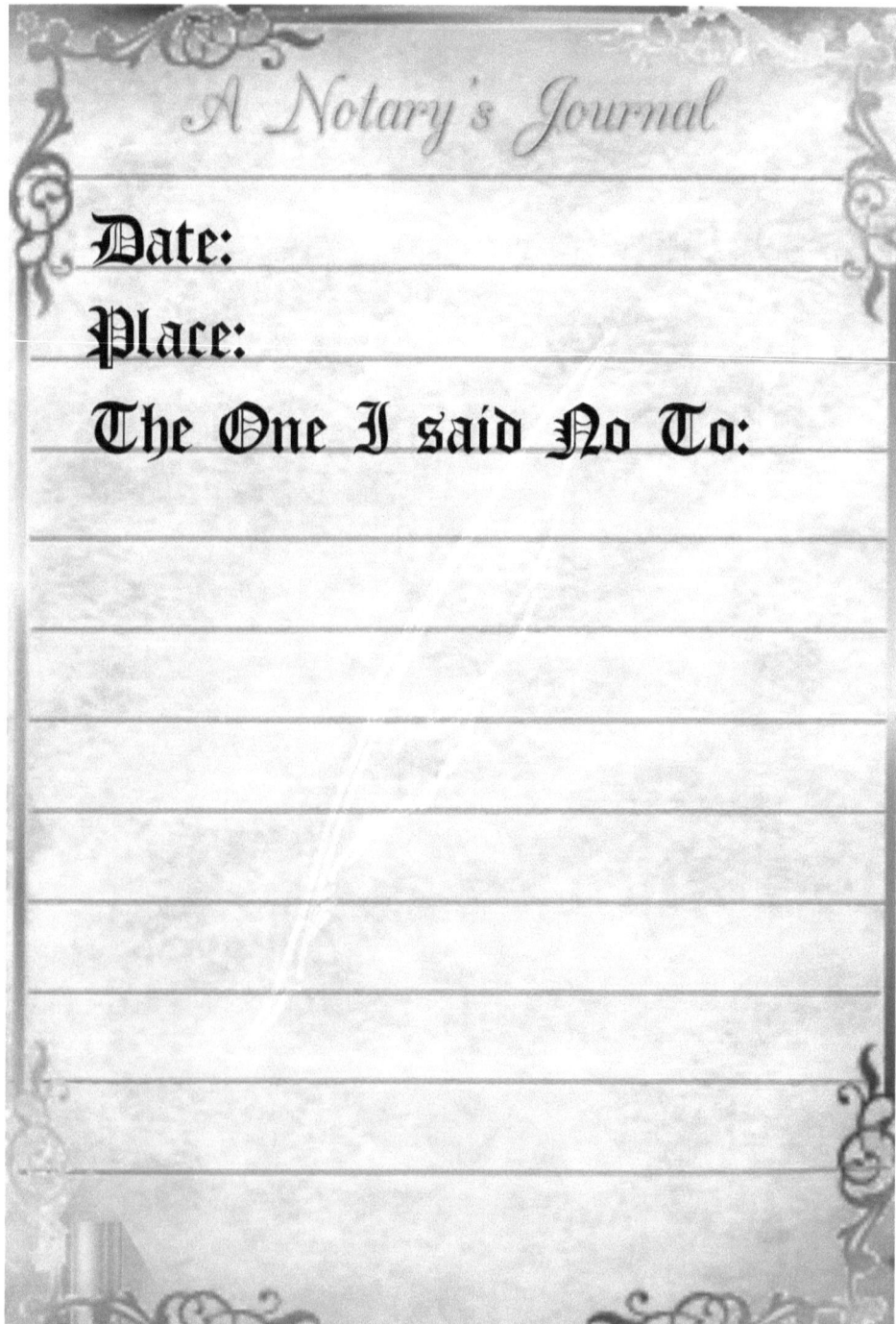

A Notary's Journal

Date:

Place:

The One I said No To:

Date:

Place:

The One I said No To:

A Notary's Journal

Date:

Place:

The One I said No To:

Date:

Place:

The One I said No To:

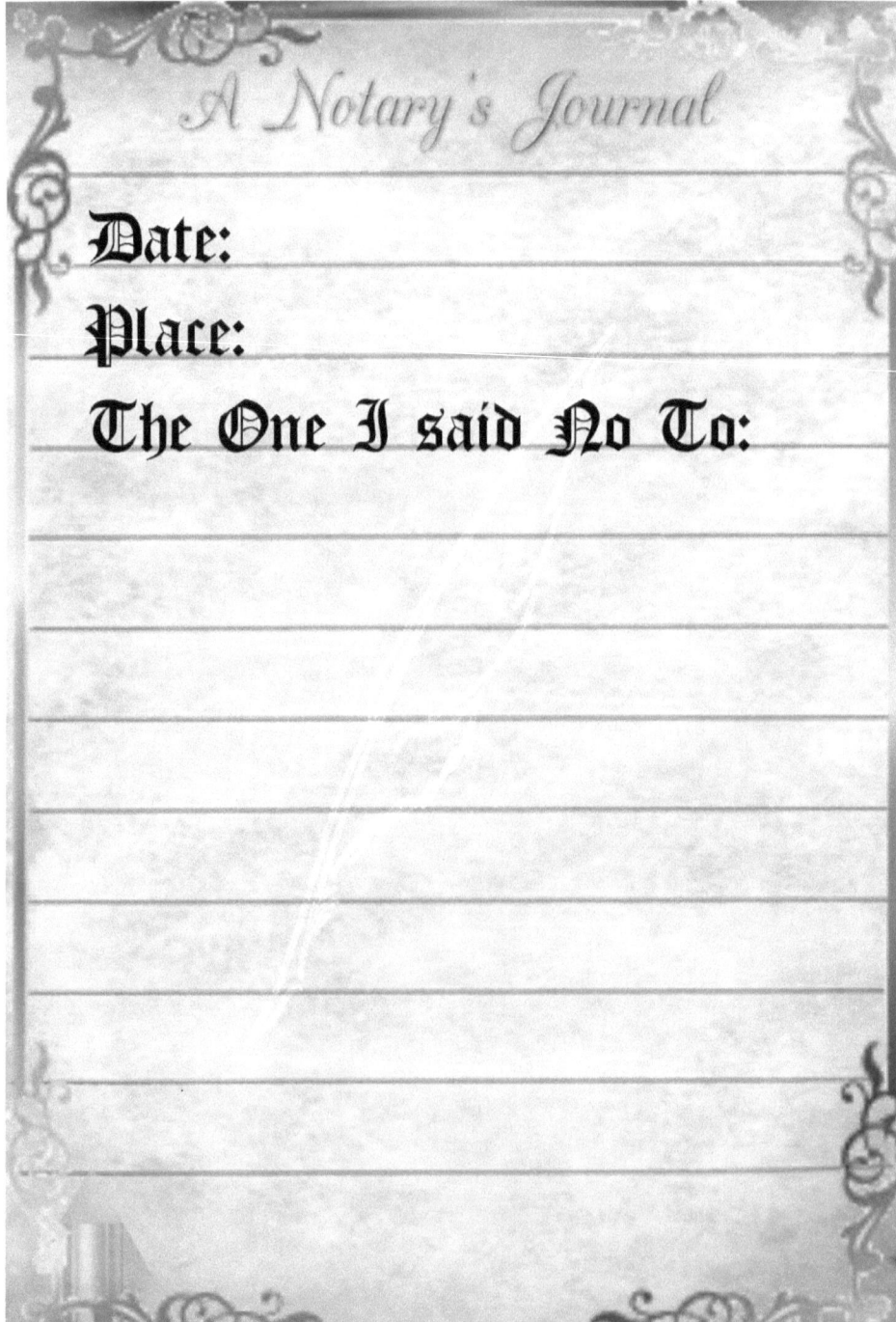

A Notary's Journal

Date:

Place:

The One I said No To:

A Notary's Journal

Date:

Place:

The One I said No To:

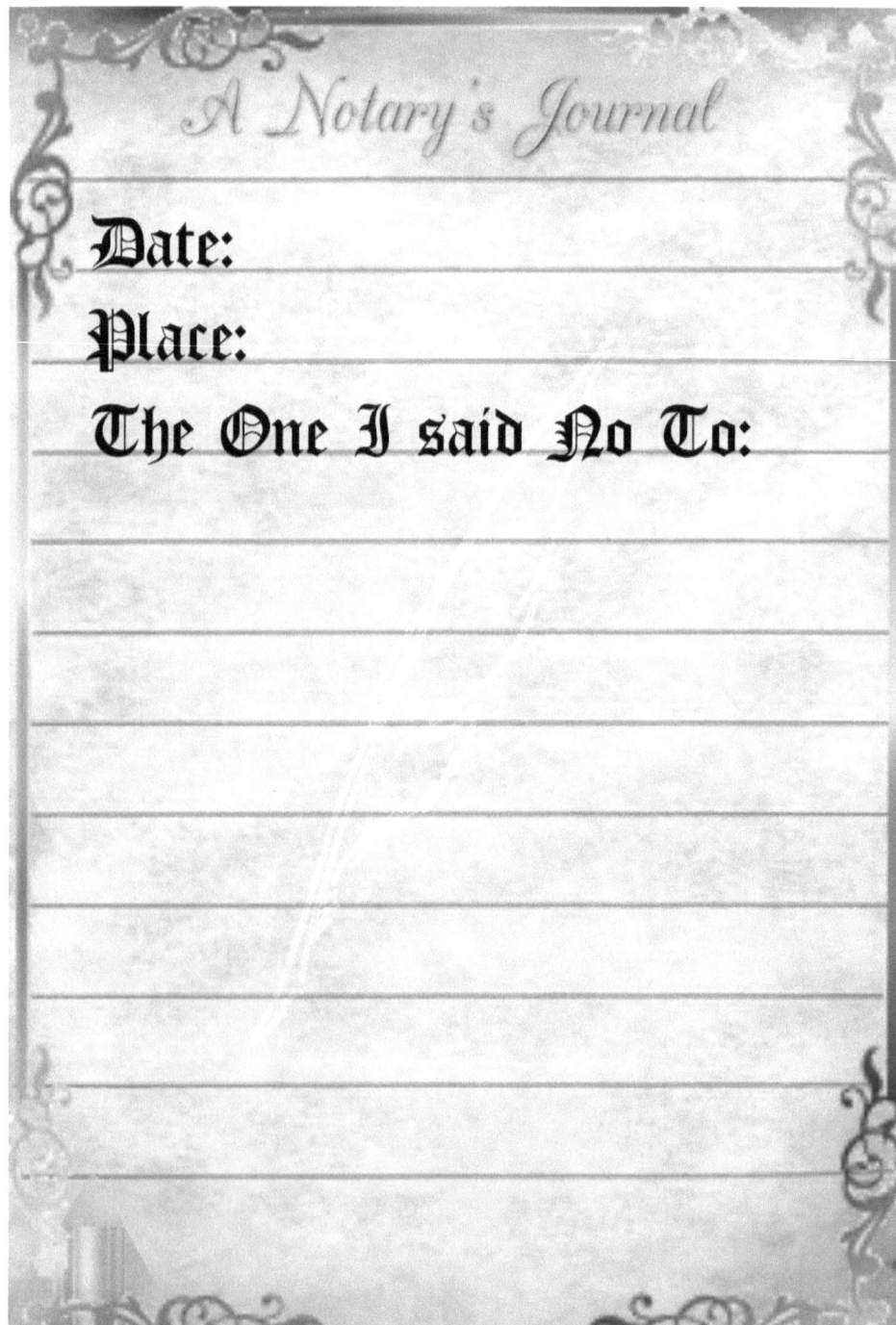

A Notary's Journal

Date:

Place:

The One I said No To:

Date:

Place:

The One I said No To:

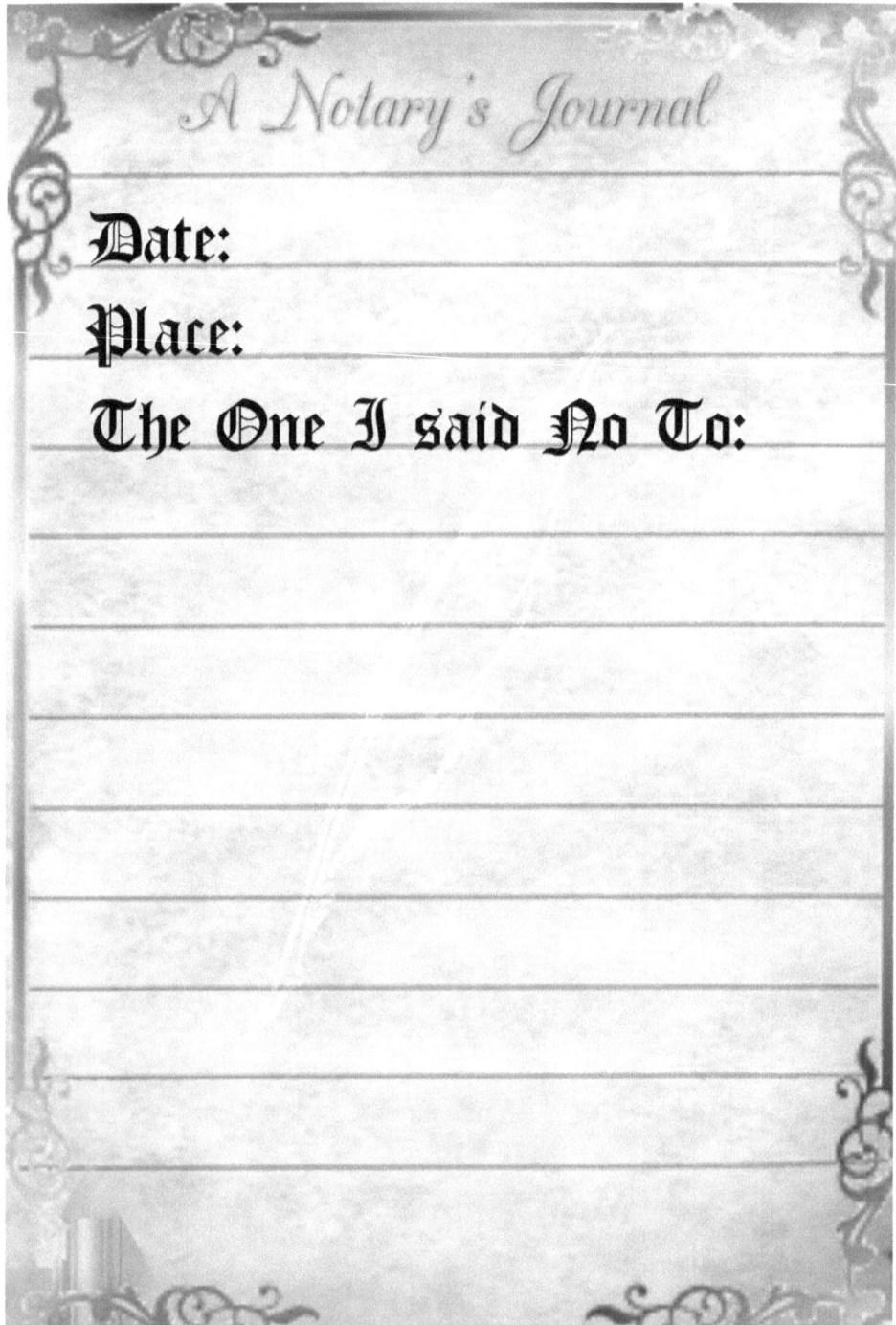

A Notary's Journal

Date:

Place:

The One I said No To:

A Notary's Journal

Date:

Place:

The One I said No To:

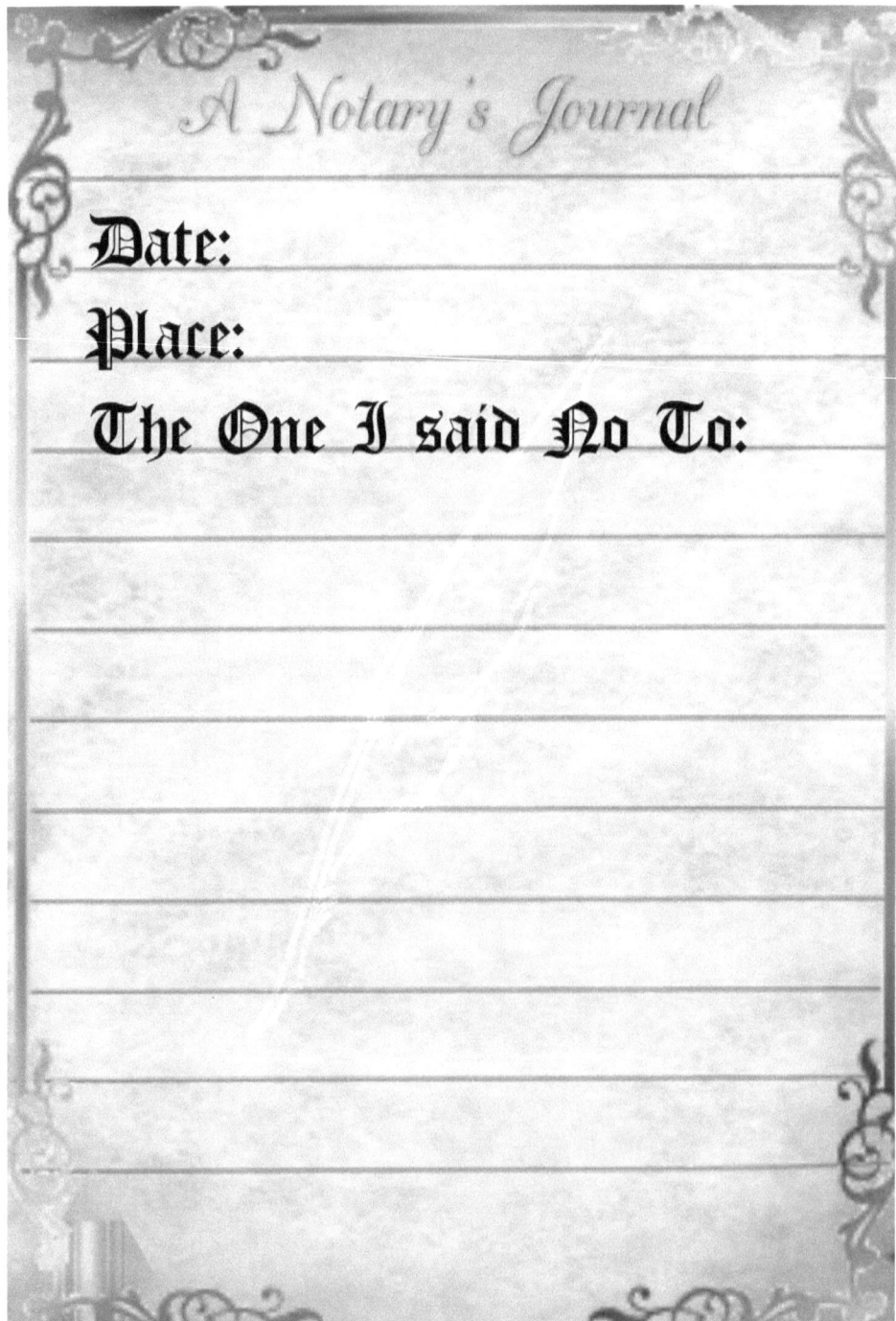

A Notary's Journal

Date:

Place:

The One I said No To:

Date:

Place:

The One I said No To:

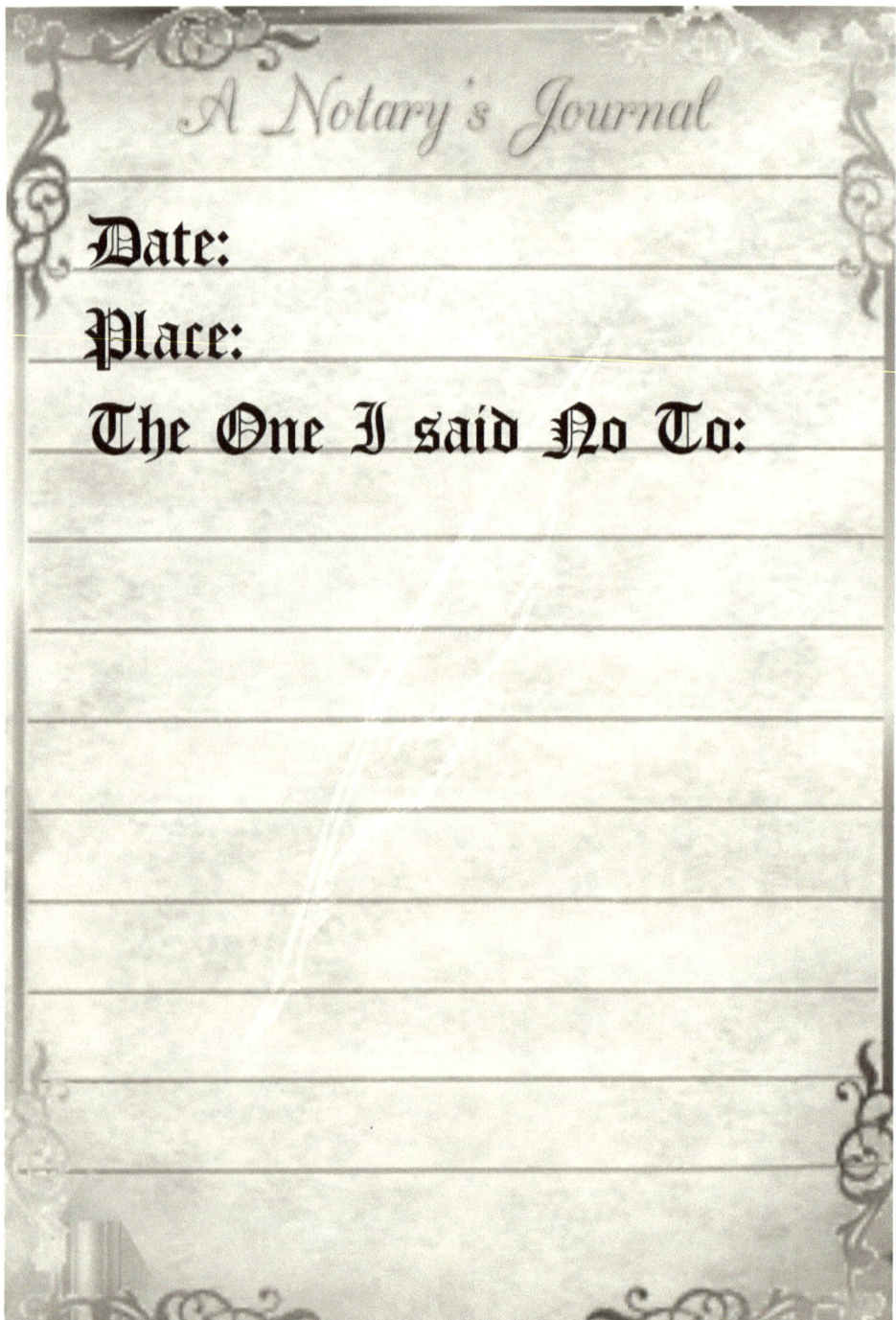

A Notary's Journal

Date:

Place:

The One I said No To:

Date:

Place:

The One I said No To:

Date:

Place:

The One I said No To:

A Notary's Journal

Date:

Place:

The One I said No To:

Date:

Place:

The One I said No To:

Date:

Place:

The One I said No To:

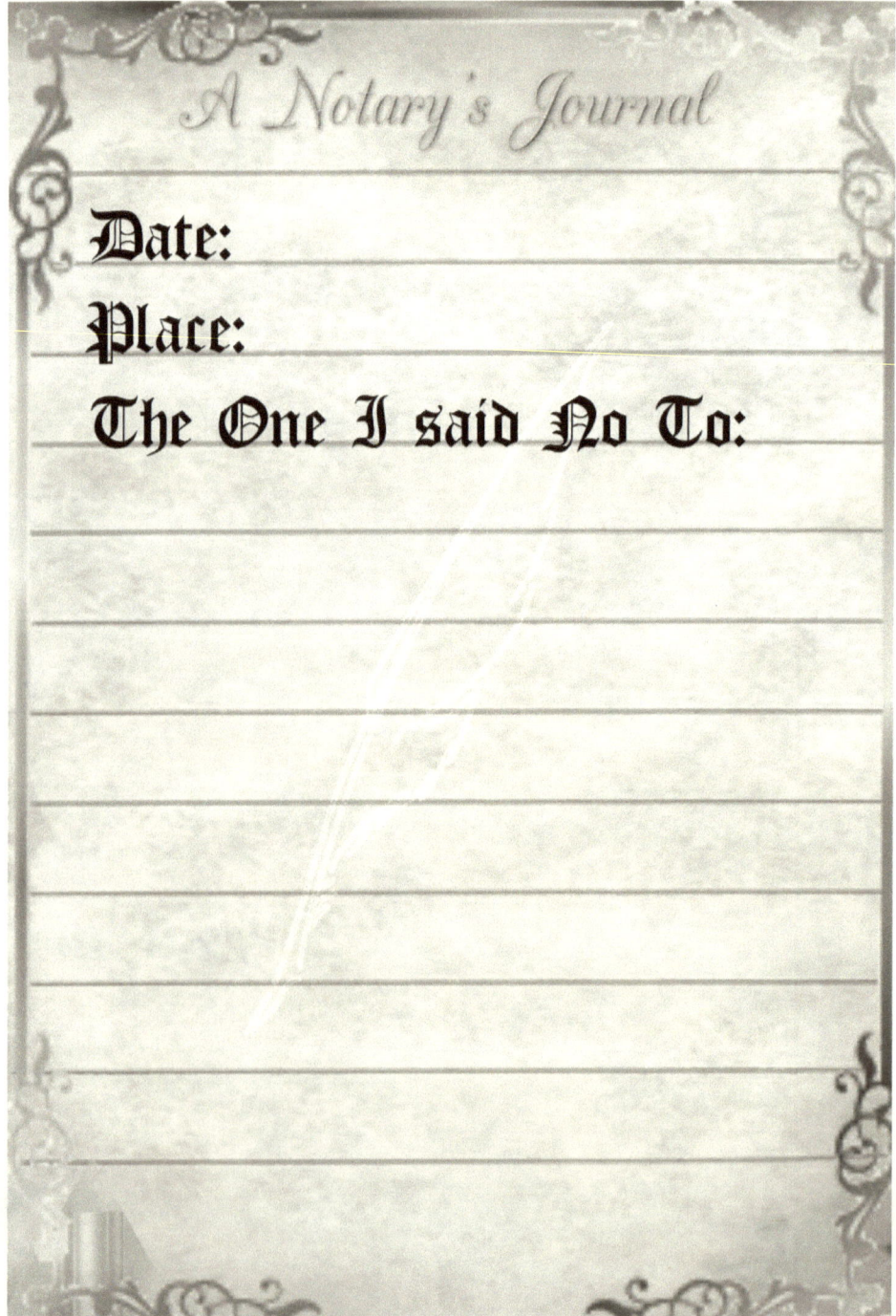

A Notary's Journal

Date:

Place:

The One I said No To:

A Notary's Journal

Date:

Place:

The One I said No To:

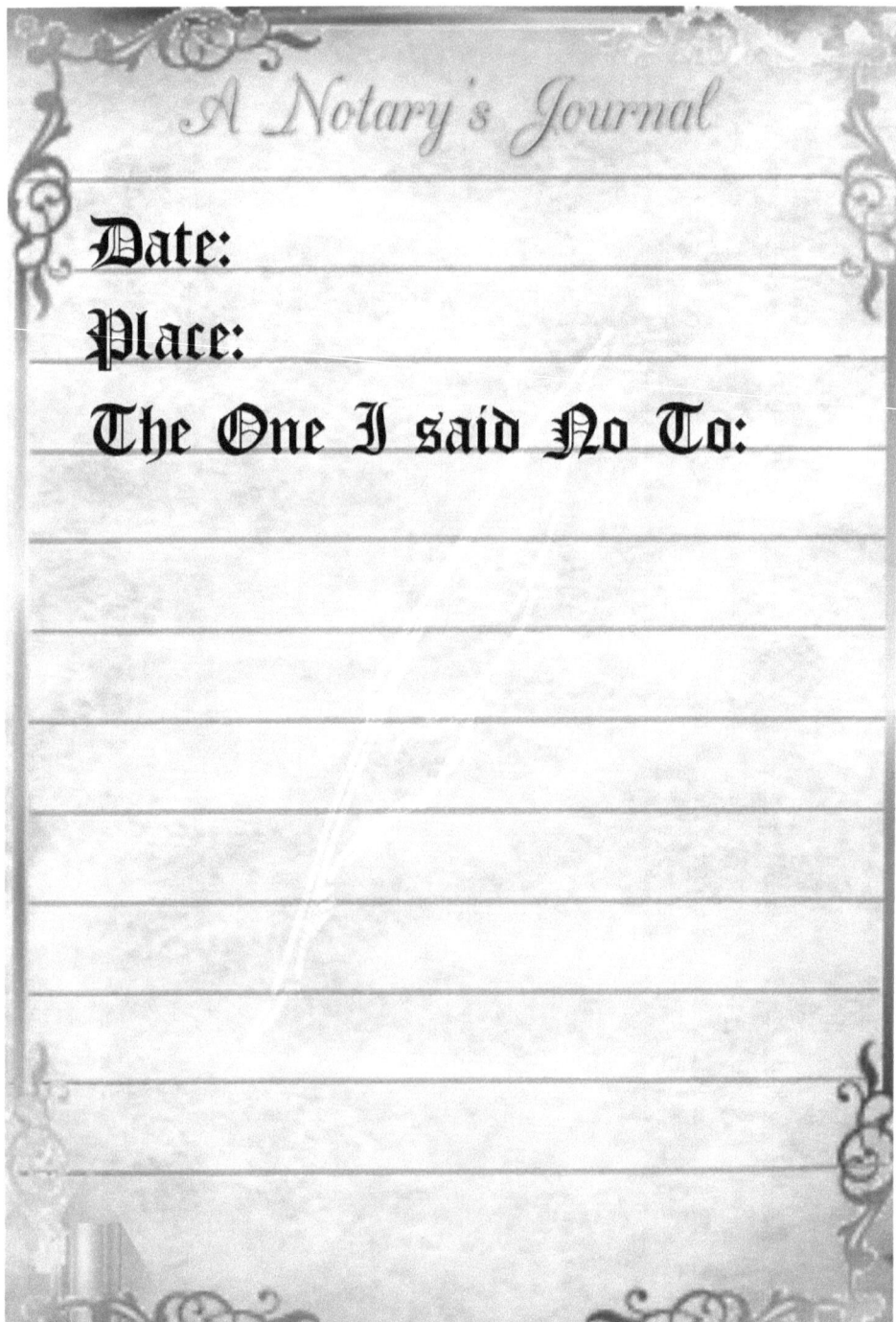

A Notary's Journal

Date:

Place:

The One I said No To:

Date:

Place:

The One I said No To:

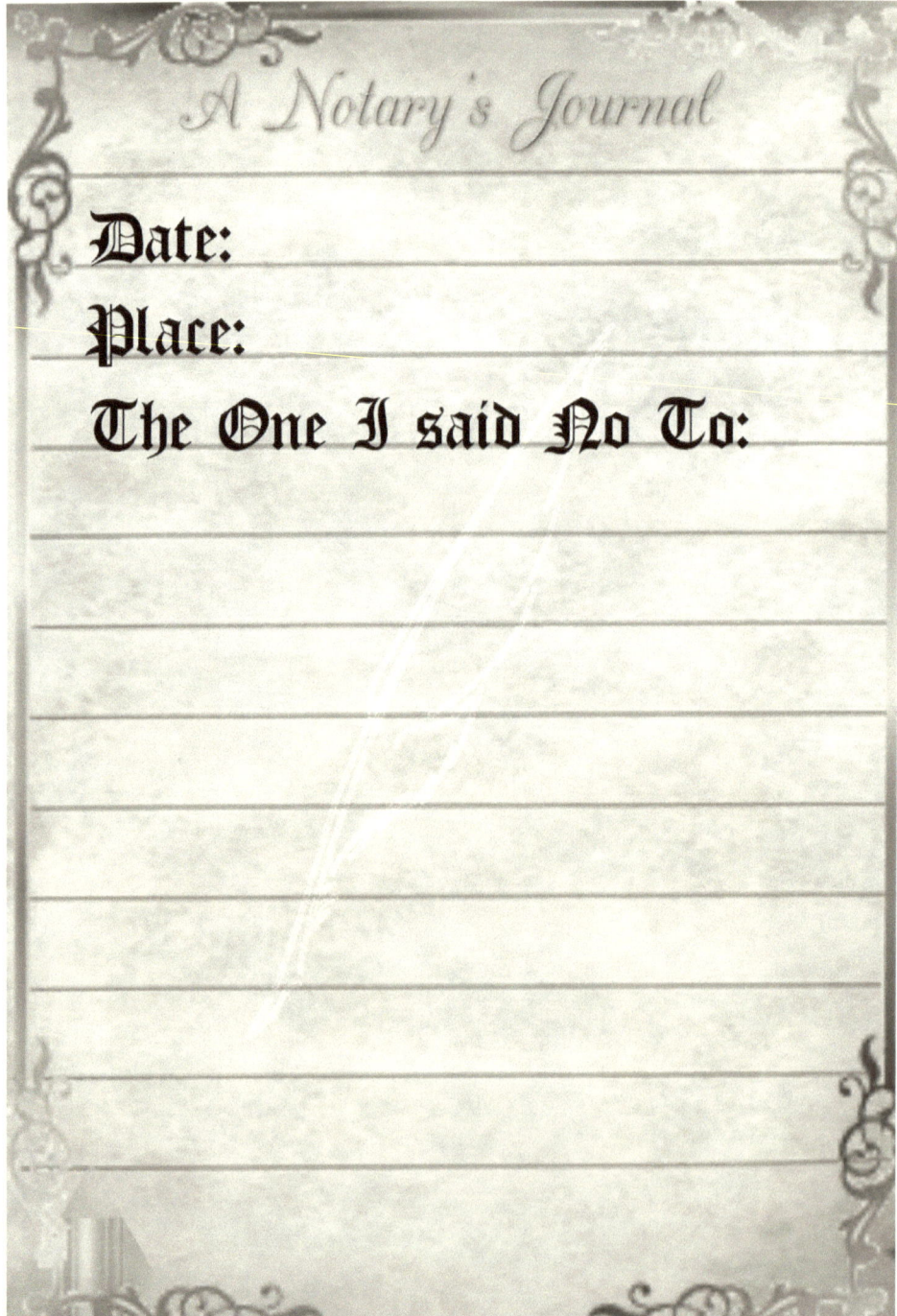

A Notary's Journal

Date:

Place:

The One I said No To:

Date:

Place:

The One I said No To:

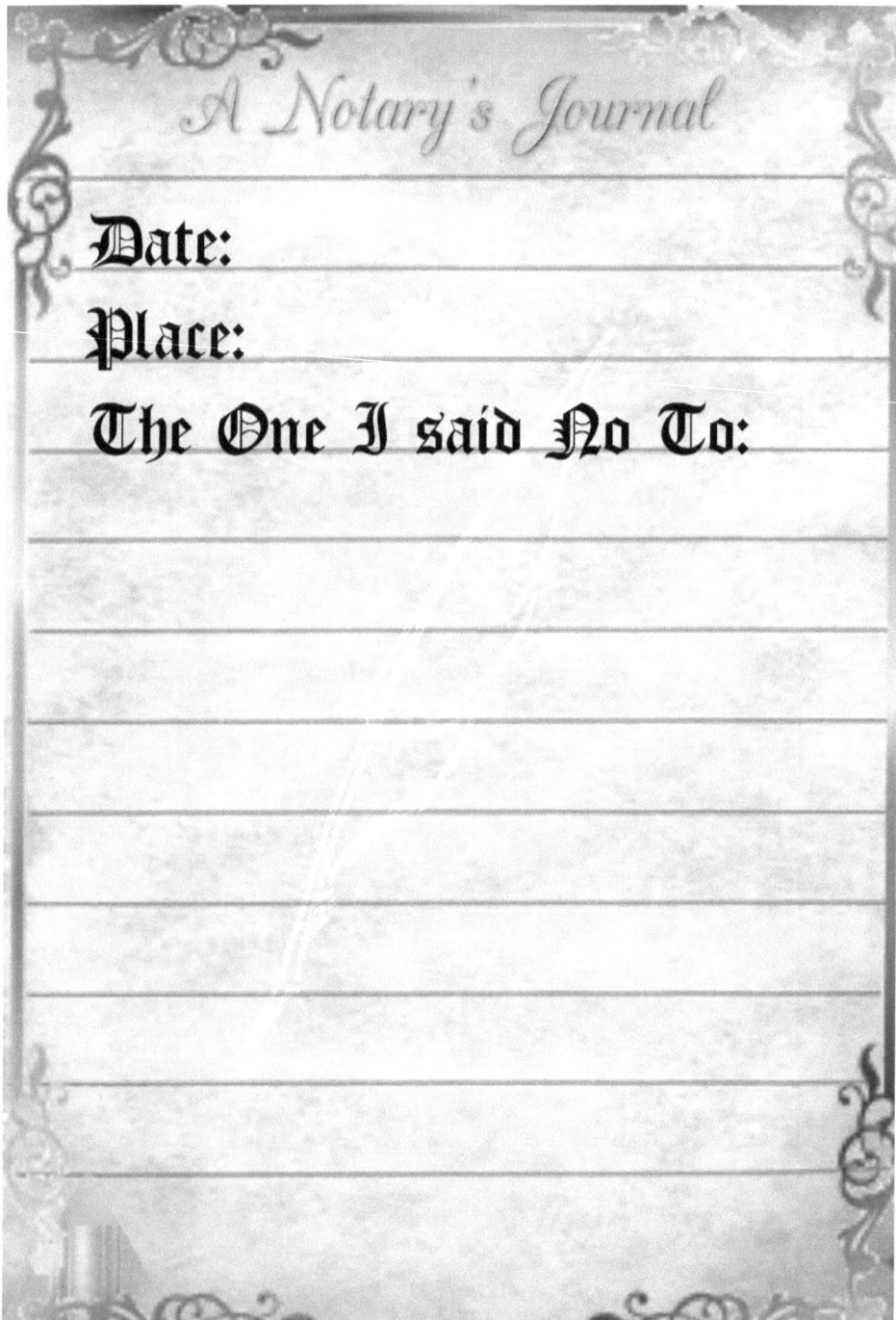

A Notary's Journal

Date:

Place:

The One I said No To:

A Notary's Journal

Date:

Place:

The One I said No To:

A Notary's Journal

Date:

Place:

The One I said No To:

Date:

Place:

The One I said No To:

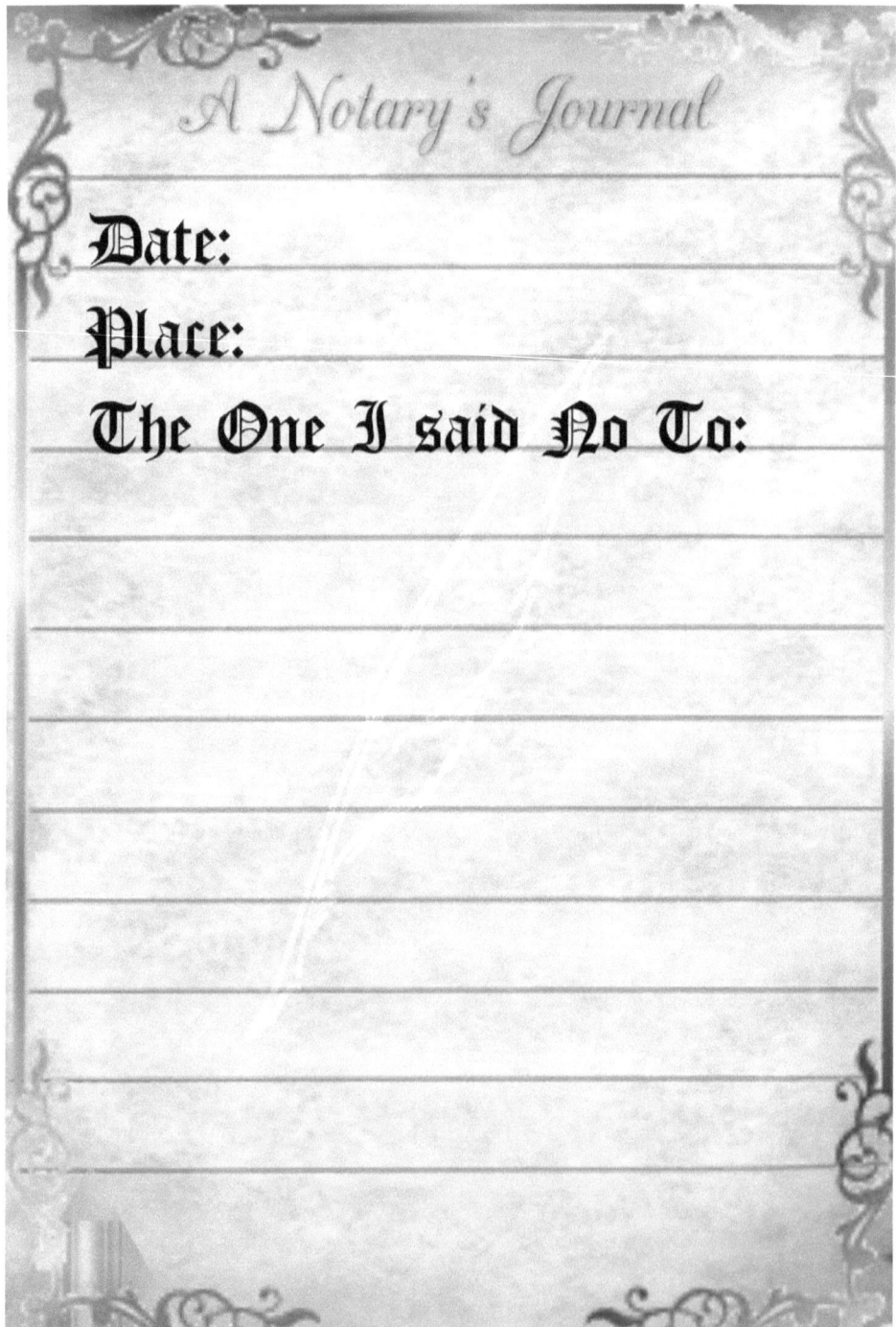

A Notary's Journal

Date:

Place:

The One I said No To:

Date:

Place:

The One I said No To:

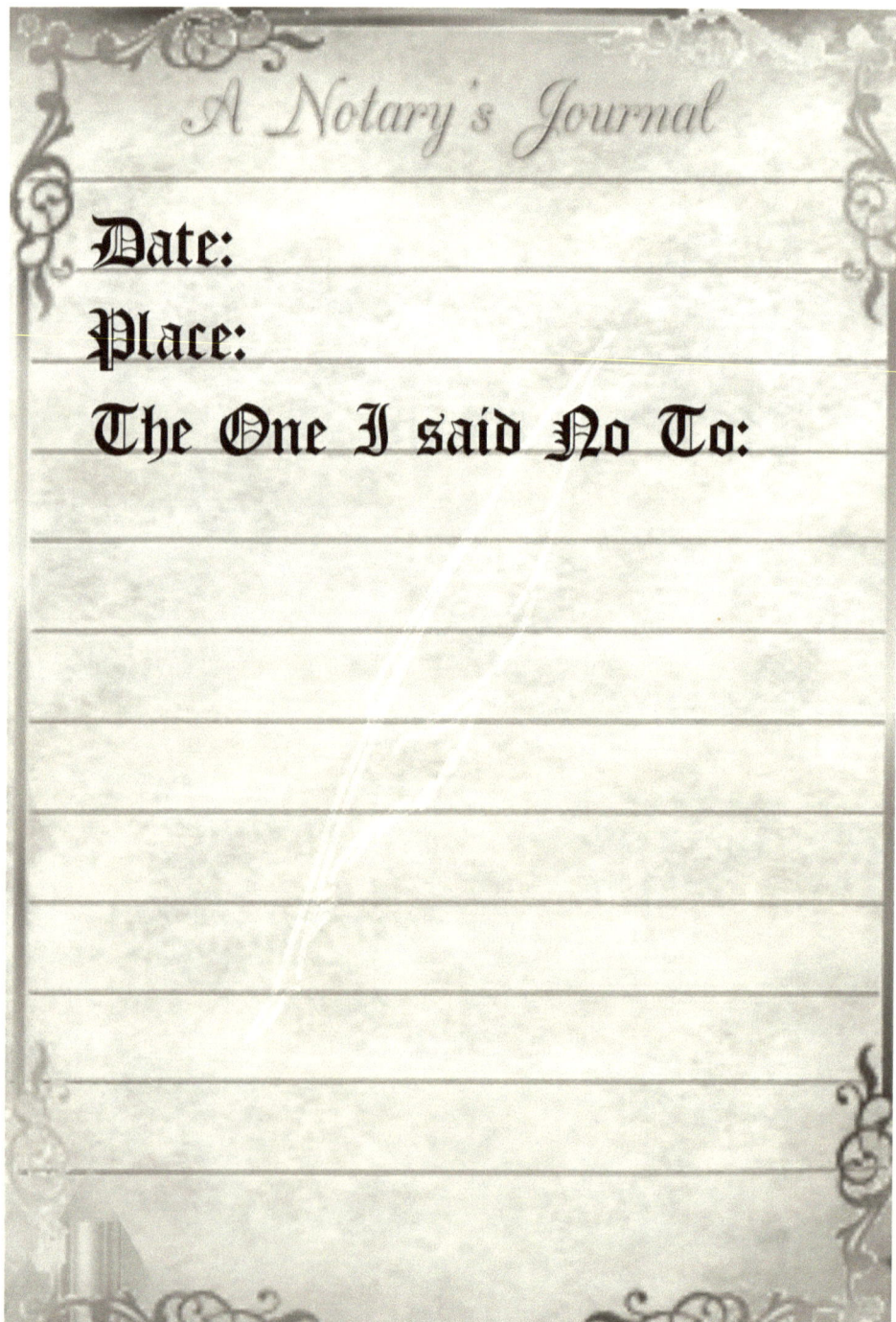

A Notary's Journal

Date:

Place:

The One I said No To:

A Notary's Journal

Date:

Place:

The One I said No To:

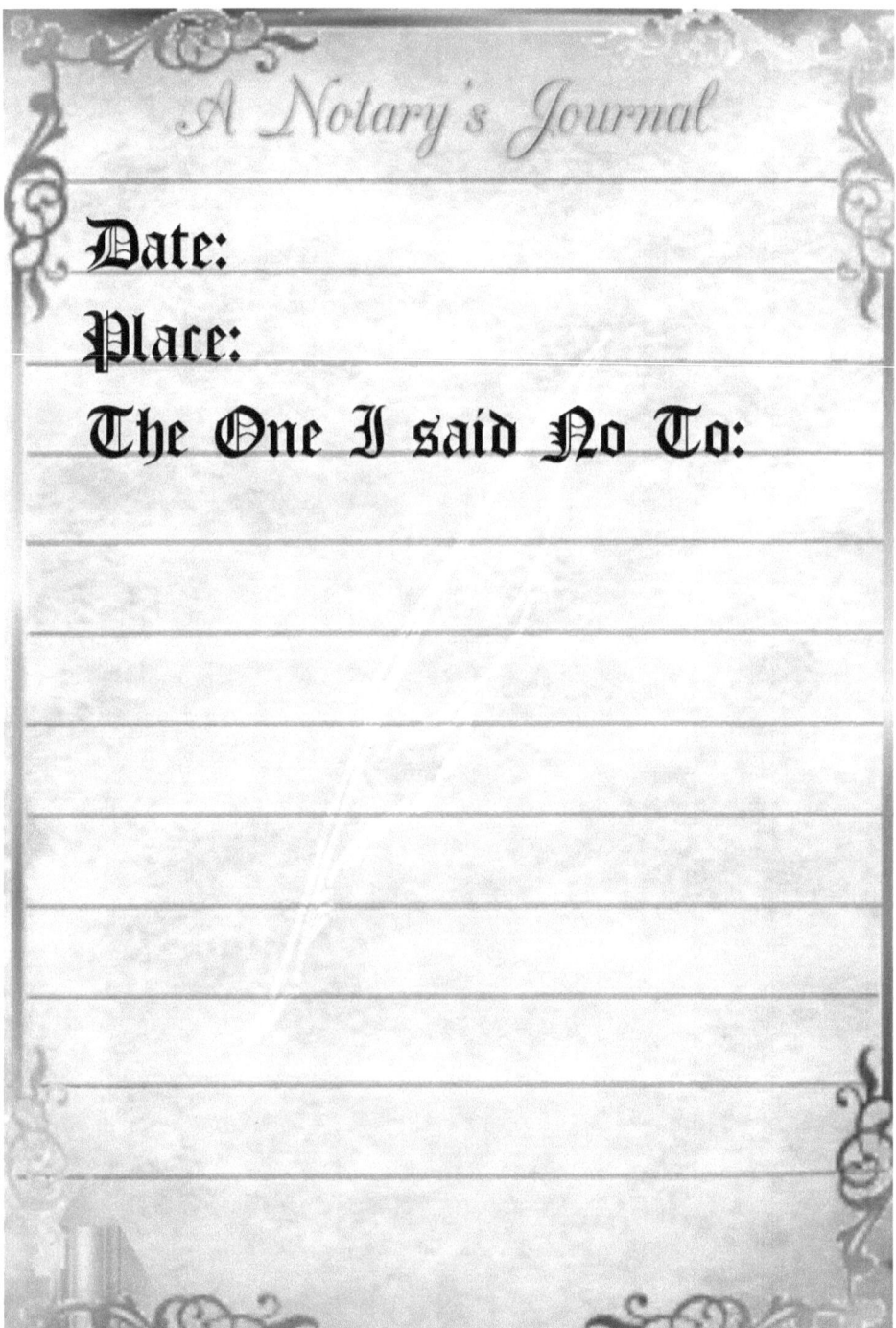

A Notary's Journal

Date:

Place:

The One I said No To:

A Notary's Journal

Date:

Place:

The One I said No To:

Date:

Place:

The One I said No To:

Date:

Place:

The One I said No To:

A Notary's Journal

Date:

Place:

The One I said No To:

A Notary's Journal

Date:

Place:

The One I said No To:

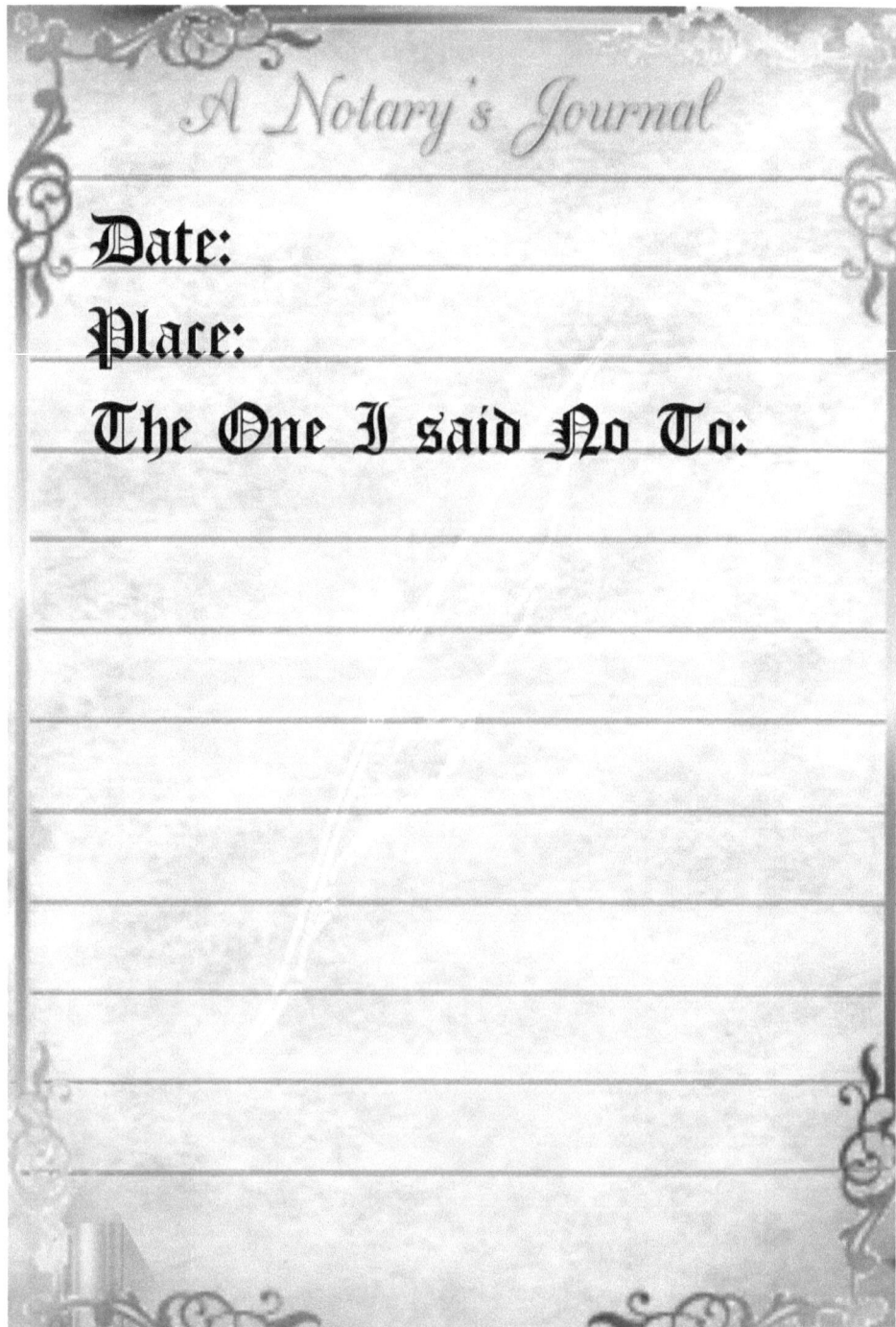

A Notary's Journal

Date:

Place:

The One I said No To:

A Notary's Journal

Date:

Place:

The One I said No To:

Date:

Place:

The One I said No To:

Date:

Place:

The One I said No To:

Date:

Place:

The One I said No To:

A Notary's Journal

Date:

Place:

The One I said No To:

A Notary's Journal

Date:

Place:

The One I said No To:

A Notary's Journal

Date:

Place:

The One I said No To:

Date:

Place:

The One I said No To:

A Notary's Journal

Date:

Place:

The One I said No To:

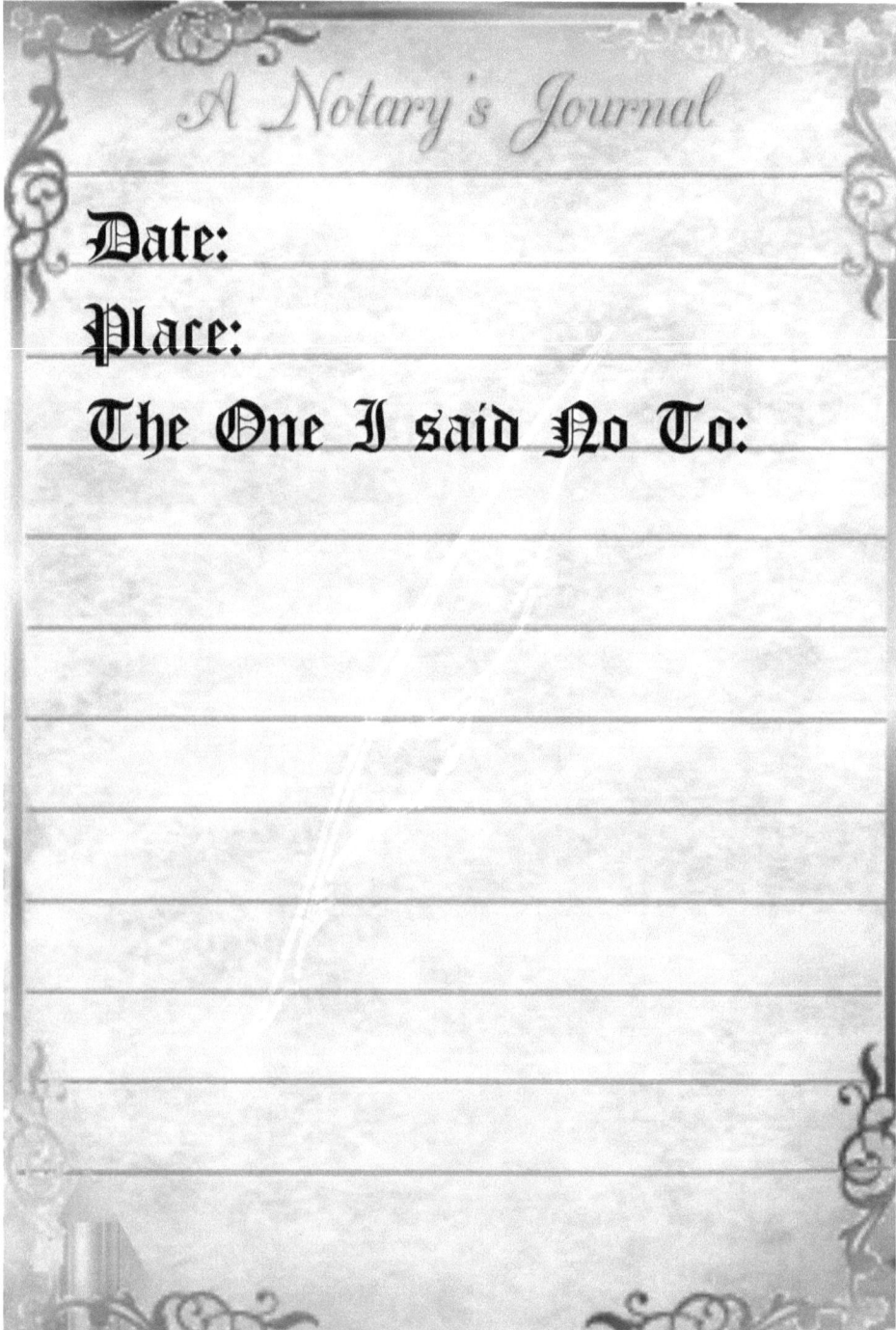

A Notary's Journal

Date:

Place:

The One I said No To:

Date:

Place:

The One I said No To:

Date:

Place:

The One I said No To:

Date:

Place:

The One I said No To:

Date:

Place:

The One I said No To:

Date:

Place:

The One I said No To:

A Notary's Journal

Date:

Place:

The One I said No To:

Date:

Place:

The One I said No To:

Date:

Place:

The One I said No To:

A Notary's Journal

Date:

Place:

The One I said No To:

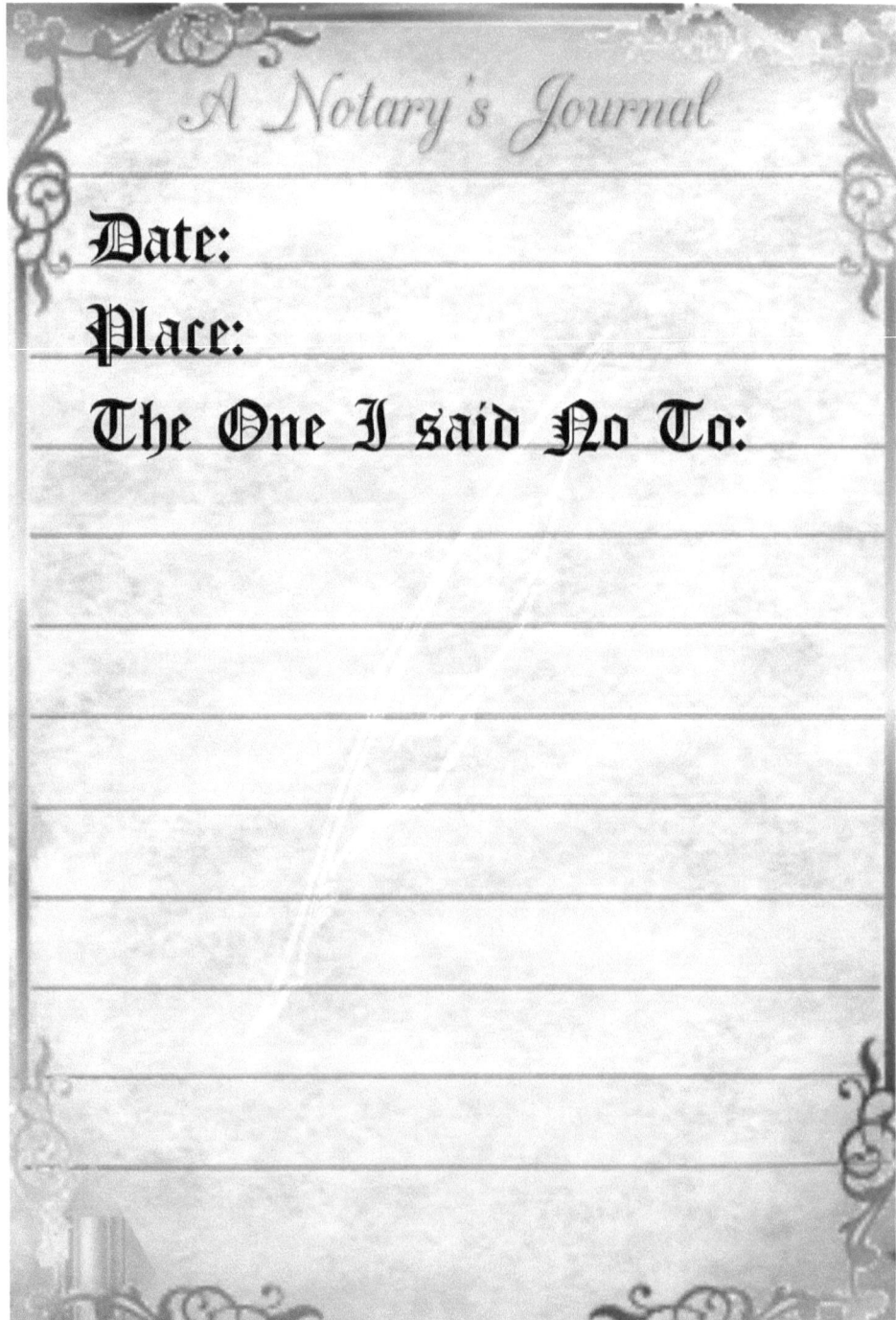

A Notary's Journal

Date:

Place:

The One I said No To:

A Notary's Journal

Date:

Place:

The One I said No To:

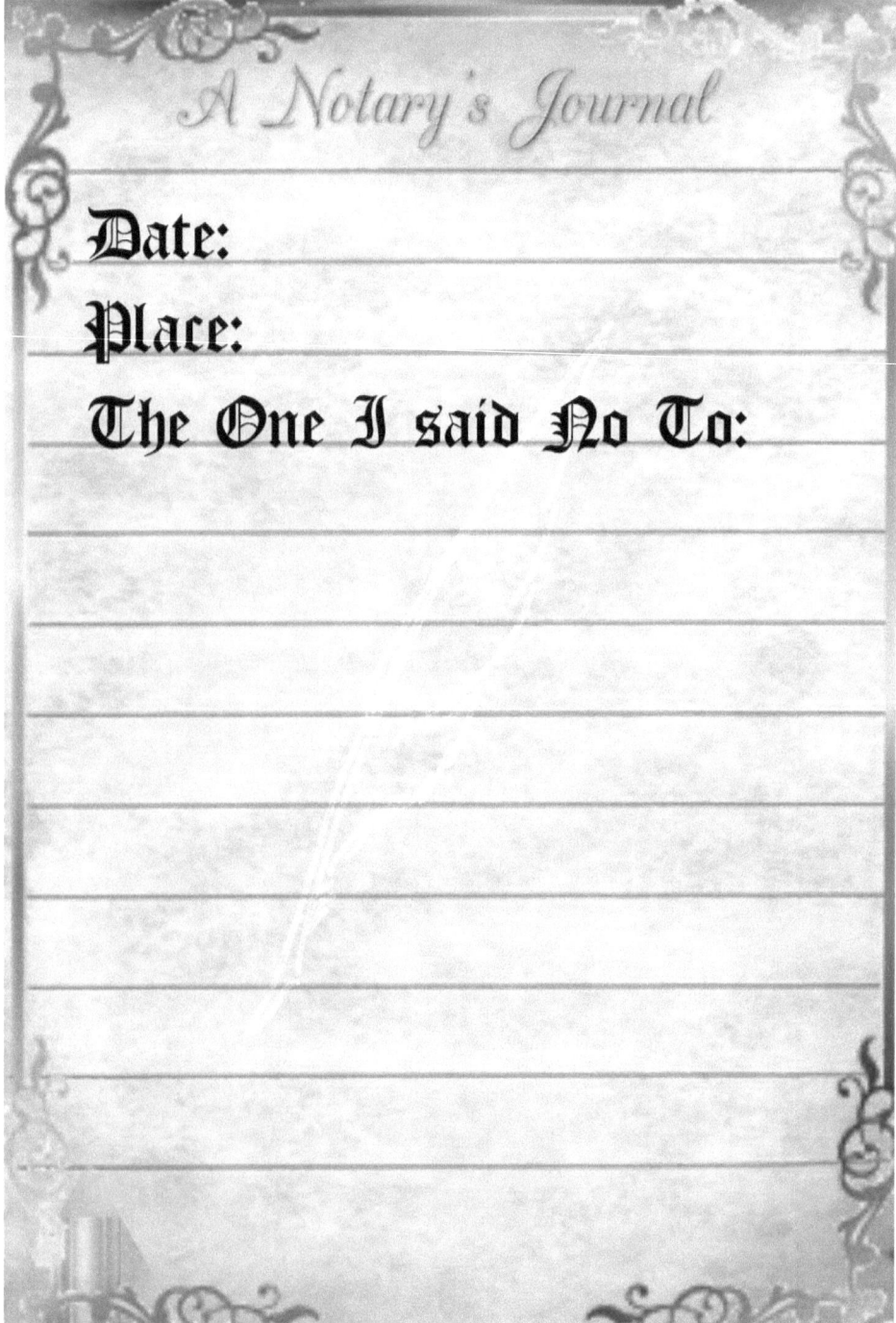

A Notary's Journal

Date:

Place:

The One I said No To:

A Notary's Journal

Date:

Place:

The One I said No To:

Date:

Place:

The One I said No To:

Date:

Place:

The One I said No To:

A Notary's Journal

Date:

Place:

The One I said No To:

A Notary's Journal

Date:

Place:

The One I said No To:

Date:

Place:

The One I said No To:

A Notary's Journal

Date:

Place:

The One I said No To:

A Notary's Journal

Date:

Place:

The One I said No To:

Date:

Place:

The One I said No To:

A Notary's Journal

Date:

Place:

The One I said No To:

A Notary's Journal

Date:

Place:

The One I said No To:

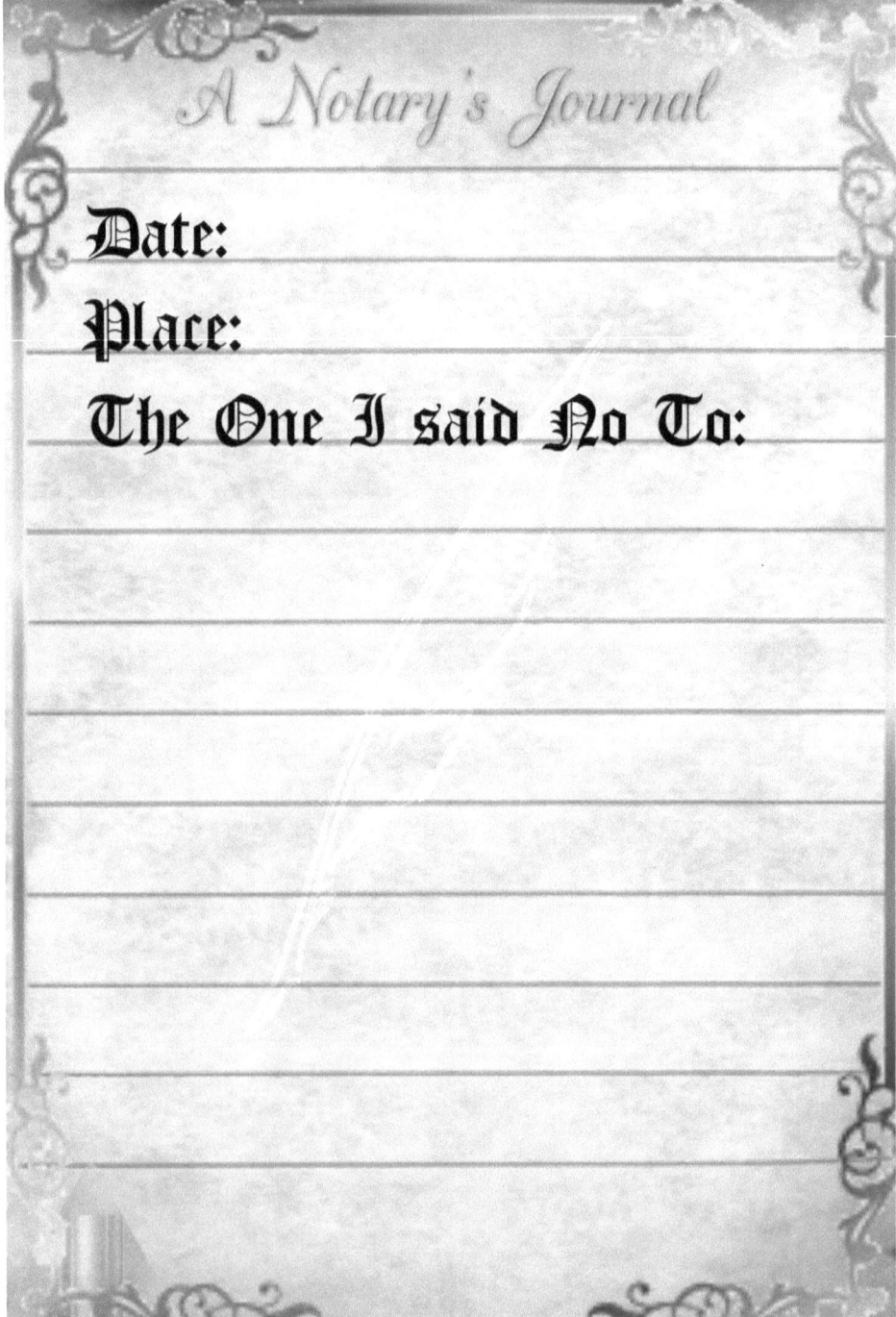

A Notary's Journal

Date:

Place:

The One I said No To:

A Notary's Journal

Date:

Place:

The One I said No To:

Date:

Place:

The One I said No To:

Date:

Place:

The One I said No To:

A Notary's Journal

www.ingramcontent.com/pod-product-compliance
Lightning Source LLC
Chambersburg PA
CBHW030902180526
45163CB00004B/1665